W9-AMN-771

Plu

My Day

by Henry Pluckrose

Gareth Stevens Publishing
A WORLD ALMANAC EDUCATION GROUP COMPANY

Please visit our web site at: **www.garethstevens.com**
For a free color catalog describing Gareth Stevens' list of high-quality books
and multimedia programs, call 1-800-542-2595 (USA) or 1-800-461-9120 (Canada).
Gareth Stevens Publishing's Fax: (414) 332-3567.

Library of Congress Cataloging-in-Publication Data

Pluckrose, Henry Arthur.
    My day / by Henry Pluckrose. — North American ed.
       p. cm. — (Let's explore)
    Includes bibliographical references and index.
    ISBN 0-8368-2963-8 (lib. bdg.)
    1. Time—Juvenile literature. [1. Time.] I. Title.
  QB209.5.P58   2001
  529'.7—dc21   2001031116

This North American edition first published in 2001 by
Gareth Stevens Publishing
A World Almanac Education Group Company
330 West Olive Street, Suite 100
Milwaukee, WI 53212 USA

This U.S. edition © 2001 by Gareth Stevens, Inc. Original edition © 2000 by Franklin Watts.
First published in 2000 by Franklin Watts, 96 Leonard Street, London, EC2A 4XD, United
Kingdom. Additional end matter © 2001 by Gareth Stevens, Inc.

Series editor: Louise John
Series designer: Jason Anscomb
Gareth Stevens editor: Monica Rausch
Gareth Stevens designer: Katherine A. Kroll

Picture credits: Steve Shott Photography cover and title page, pp. 9, 10, 12, 28, 31, and
all clock photography; Ray Moller Photography p. 4; Image Bank p. 6 (Britt Erlanson);
© Bob Daemmrich/The Image Works p. 19; Bubbles p. 20 (Ian West); Harry Cory-Wright
p. 23; Robert Harding p. 24; Eye Ubiquitous p. 27 (Kevin Wilton); Franklin Watts stock
photography pp. 15, 17.

With thanks to our models: David Kimberley, José Ballesteros, Victoria Harris, and
Sam Stephenson.

Printed in the United States of America

1 2 3 4 5 6 7 8 9 05 04 03 02 01

Contents

Are you still asleep? It is morning —
time to wake up! What will you do
with your time today?

7:00

Remember to make your bed.
Then it is time to wash your face,
comb your hair, and get dressed.

7:15

Are you hungry? It is breakfast time. What do you like to eat for breakfast?

7:30

10

After breakfast, remember to brush your teeth before you go to school.

7:45

Now it is time to leave for school. Pack your books, papers, and pencils in your school bag. Do not forget your lunch!

8:00

If you get to school early, you might have time to play before your lessons begin.

8:30

In the morning, you might have lessons in reading, writing, or mathematics. You also might have time to work on a computer.

9:00

Now it is lunch time. After lunch, you will have more time to play. What games can you play on the playground?

12:00

In the afternoon, you may visit the school library. What kinds of books do you like to read in the library?

2:00

When school is over, it is time to go home — unless your mom takes you shopping first.

3:00

You might have time to play video games before supper, but you might have to help set the table, too.

5:00

After supper, fill up the bathtub with warm, soapy water — it is time for a bath. What toys do you play with in the tub?

7:00

Now it is time for a bedtime story.
Then say "Good night!" and snuggle
down to sleep.

8:00

It is morning again and a new day.
But you do not have school today!
It is Saturday. What will you do
with all your time?

9:00

Index

More Books to Read

Jamal's Busy Day. Feeling Good (series).
   Wade Hudson and Veronica F. Ellis (Just Us Books)
What's the Time? Lara Tankel Holtz (DK Publishing)
*Why I Will Never Ever Ever Ever Have Enough Time to
   Read This Book.* Remy Charlip (Tricycle Press)